MINDFULNESS WHILE

EATING

PRISCILLA AN

T0009916

childsworld.com

Published by The Child's World®
800-599-READ · www.childsworld.com

Photography Credits
Photographs ©: Anna Stills/Shutterstock Images, cover,
1, 14–15, 17, 18, 20; Jeni Foto/Shutterstock Images, 3;
iStockphoto, 4–5; Drazen Zigic/Shutterstock Images, 6–7,
8, 11, 13; Shutterstock Images, 22

ISBN Information
9781503869592 (Reinforced Library Binding)
9781503880900 (Portable Document Format)
9781503882218 (Online Multi-user eBook)
9781503883529 (Electronic Publication)
9781645498650 (Paperback)

LCCN 2022951257

Printed in the United States of America

Priscilla An is a children's book editor and author. She lives in Minnesota with her rabbit and likes to practice mindfulness through yoga.

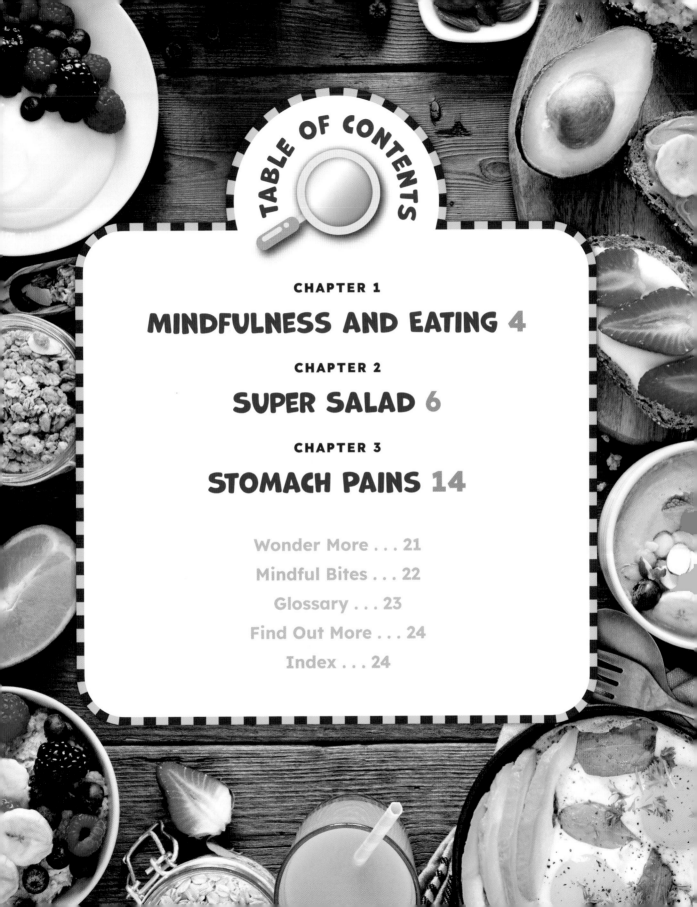

TABLE OF CONTENTS

MINDFULNESS AND EATING

Eating is an everyday **routine**. Sometimes, people do not pay attention to what they are eating. They might not think about how eating can affect their bodies. Mindfulness is when people are able to notice their thoughts, feelings, and surroundings. Being mindful while eating can help people pay attention to what they eat. People can notice when they are hungry and when they are full. Practicing mindful eating can help people enjoy their food more.

Eating ice cream with friends can be a special treat.

CHAPTER 2

SUPER SALAD

A delicious smell fills the house. Jocelyn's parents are almost done making **brunch**. Her dad calls her over. Jocelyn runs to the dining room table. On her plate are salad, eggs, sausages, and bacon. Jocelyn frowns as she sits. She likes sausages, eggs, and bacon. But she does not like salad.

Many families enjoy spending time together over a meal.

Some people do not like to eat vegetables.

Jocelyn takes a bite of her bacon. It is juicy and crispy. "Mmmm, this tastes good!" Jocelyn uses her fork to push the salad to the edges of her plate.

Jocelyn's mom sees that Jocelyn is not eating her salad. "Vegetables and fruits have vitamins that are good for you," she says. "Vitamins help make our bodies stronger." She picks up a tomato with her fork and gives it to Jocelyn. Jocelyn closes her mouth.

"Tomatoes taste bad," she says. She crosses her arms. Jocelyn does not remember the last time she ate a tomato. But she knows she did not like it.

"Why do you like eating bacon?" her mom asks.

"Because it's **savory** and crunchy," Jocelyn says. She eats another bite of bacon. "It even tastes a little sweet!"

"Tomatoes can taste sweet, too," her mom says. "Try eating the tomato like you are eating bacon. Chew it slowly. Notice its texture. Think about the vitamins it gives your body."

"You know, our sense of taste changes over time," Jocelyn's dad says. "Just because you didn't like it before does not mean you won't like it now."

"Fine. I can try *one*." Jocelyn takes a bite of tomato. It bursts in her mouth! It is very juicy. The tomato tastes sweet.

Tomatoes have a lot of important vitamins.

It is not as tasty as the bacon. But it is much better than she remembers.

"If you want, I can also sprinkle some bacon on your salad." Jocelyn's mom smiles. "Balance is important. Sometimes putting something you really like on a salad can make the salad easier to eat."

"Yes, please!" Jocelyn squeals. "That sounds tasty!"

"I am so proud of you for trying something new!" Jocelyn's dad gives her a high-five. When Jocelyn tries the salad with bacon, she thinks it tastes delicious. She had always thought salad had only vegetables and fruits. But now she knows that it can include different ingredients. Being mindful of what she ate helped her think differently about eating salads. Jocelyn imagines working in the kitchen with her parents. They can come up with all kinds of new recipes together! She cannot wait to try something new.

VEGETABLES AND FRUITS

Vegetables and fruits are packed with important vitamins. For example, grapefruits have a lot of vitamin C. Vitamin C can help people heal faster when they get sick. It also keeps bones and blood vessels healthy.

People can practice mindfulness while preparing and eating food.

STOMACH PAINS

Eli is having a big birthday party. His cousins and grandparents came over for dinner. His family made all his favorite dishes. His dad baked a strawberry cake for dessert. Eli cannot wait to eat everything.

Family celebrations often include food.

Eli loads his plate with delicious food. First, Eli eats some bread. The bread is buttery and a little crispy, just how he likes it! Eli plans to try some potatoes next. But he notices that his cousins are already almost done eating.

"After we eat, do you want to play soccer?" Benny asks. "I brought a new ball for you."

"Yeah!" Eli says. He cannot wait to play. But he needs dinner first. Eli shovels several pieces of potato into his mouth. He takes a drink to wash them down quickly. Then he eats a few bites of salad. Eli's stomach starts to hurt a little bit, but he ignores it. He had saved the chicken for last. But just as he takes a bite, his three cousins stand up. Their plates are empty.

It is important for people to chew when they eat.

"Come outside when you're done!" Benny says.

Eli smiles and waves. He feels like he needs to eat faster. He starts shoving the chicken into his mouth. But before Eli finishes, his stomach gurgles. It really hurts now.

"Ow!" Eli yells.

Parents can give good advice.

INDIGESTION

Indigestion is when the stomach has a hard time digesting food. It can cause stomachaches and make people feel sick. It happens when people eat too quickly or eat too much food.

Eli's mom comes over. "Are you feeling all right?" she asks. Eli shakes his head.

"My stomach is burning." Eli scrunches his face and holds his belly.

"It looks like you were eating too fast," his mom says. "It takes time for your stomach to **communicate** with your brain. When you eat too quickly, you might eat more than your stomach can handle. You need to chew and swallow every bite instead of gulping your food down. You are less likely to **choke** that way. It also gives your body time to **digest** and tell you if you are full."

Eli sighs. His mom was right. He had eaten so quickly that he ignored the first time his stomach started hurting. "I wanted to eat cake, too. But I guess I'm too full now," he says sadly.

The birthday cake is often the highlight of the party.

Eli's mom laughs. "How about I call your cousins in so we can all play a board game together? That will give everyone a chance for their stomachs to digest before we eat cake."

"OK!" Eli nods. His stomach is hurting less now. But he knows that continuing to rest is a good idea. He does not like the way he feels. He decides that he will be more mindful when he eats. If he does that, he is less likely to get stomachaches.

WONDER MORE

Wondering about New Information

How much did you know about the importance of eating fruits and vegetables before reading this book? What new information did you learn? Write down two new facts that this book taught you. Was the new information surprising? Why or why not?

Wondering How It Matters

What is one way being mindful while eating relates to your life? How do you think being mindful while eating relates to other kids' lives?

Wondering Why

Some foods are better for your body than others. Why do you think it is important to know the difference? How might knowing this affect your life?

Ways to Keep Wondering

Learning about mindfulness while eating can be a complex topic. After reading this book, what questions do you have about it? What can you do to learn more about mindfulness?

MINDFUL BITES

Try this mindfulness activity when you eat a snack.

1. See: What does the food look like? What color is it?

2. Smell: What does the food smell like? Is it sweet or savory?

3. Touch: What does the food feel like? Does it feel bumpy or smooth? Is it mushy?

4. Taste: Put the food in your mouth. What does it taste like before you chew? How about after chewing? Is it sour? Is it bitter?

5. Hear: When you chew, what sounds does the food make? Is it crunchy?

GLOSSARY

brunch (BRUHNCH) Brunch is a meal late in the morning that has both breakfast and lunch foods. Jocelyn's mom made bacon and salad for brunch.

choke (CHOHK) To choke is when a person cannot breathe because something is stuck in her throat. Eli's mom tells Eli to chew slowly so he does not choke on his food.

communicate (kuh-MYOO-ni-kayt) To communicate is to pass on information. When a person is hungry, the stomach can communicate to the brain that it is time to eat.

digest (dy-JEST) To digest is to break down food. Eli took a break from eating so his stomach could digest his food.

routine (roo-TEEN) A routine is something that a person does regularly. Eating three meals a day is a daily routine for many people.

savory (SAY-vuh-ree) When a food is savory, it tastes salty or spicy. Jocelyn likes eating bacon because it is crunchy and savory.

FIND OUT MORE

In the Library

An, Priscilla. *Mindfulness with Family.*
Parker, CO: The Child's World, 2024.

Dinmont, Kerry. *Alex Eats the Rainbow: A Book about Healthy Eating.* Parker, CO: The Child's World, 2018.

Lawler, Jean C. *Experience Nutrition: How the Food You Eat Makes You Feel.*
South Egremont, MA: Red Chair Press, 2019.

On the Web

Visit our website for links about mindfulness while eating:

childsworld.com/links

Note to Parents, Caregivers, Teachers, and Librarians: We routinely verify our Web links to make sure they are safe and active sites. So encourage your readers to check them out!

INDEX